The Travelers and the Bear

Retold by Lynne Benton
Illustrated by Aleksey & Olga Ivanov

A Harcourt Achieve Imprint

www.Rigby.com
1-800-531-5015

Jack was a woodsman who lived alone in a small log cabin on the edge of a great pine forest. He happily spent his time chopping wood to sell, catching rabbits to eat, and fishing from the bridge over the river.

But Jack never went into the heart of the forest because he knew that bears lived there, and bears were dangerous.

One day his old school friend Gordon, who lived in the busy city, telephoned to ask if he could come and stay. Gordon said that he'd heard about a great white moose that was supposed to live deep in the forest.

"I thought we'd go and track it down. A picture of it would sell for lots of money!"

"But there are dangerous bears in the forest," said Jack.

Gordon laughed. "Oh, bears don't scare me! I've met lions, tigers, and elephants on my travels, and I've never been harmed. I'm not worried about meeting a bear, so I'll see you on Saturday."

Jack sighed as he replied, "OK."

On Saturday Gordon arrived at Jack's cabin. He was wearing a fancy suit and carrying a fancy camera.

"I should get a good picture of the moose with this camera," he said.

"OK," said Jack, "but we have to watch out for bears."

"Don't worry!" Gordon boasted. "You'll be safe with me because I'm used to being around wild animals!"

So they set off into the forest.

It was dark and gloomy among the pine trees, and the tall straight trunks seemed to stretch right up to the pale sky. Jack thought they looked like the bars of a jail.

Just then Gordon noticed some tracks on the path. "Look!" he said excitedly. "Are those moose tracks?"

Jack shook his head and replied, "Those are badger tracks. Moose have hooves, not paws."

"Of course," said Gordon, turning red. "I knew that. I was just testing you!" Gordon said nothing then for a while.

They kept walking until they were deep into the forest. The trees grew even closer together as if they were barring the way. It was gloomier than ever, and there were still no signs of moose tracks.

At last Jack said, "I don't think we're going to catch sight of your moose now, so we'd better turn back."

Gordon grinned. "You're only scared we'll meet a bear!" he mocked.

He was right, but Jack didn't want to admit it, especially since Gordon didn't seem to be scared of anything. "I just think we should turn back now, before we get lost," he said.

Gordon sighed. "OK," he agreed, "if you insist."

But at that moment, a dark shadow
moved across their path.

Suddenly the creature stopped, sniffed the air, and turned its head until it was looking straight at them.

It was a huge grizzly bear!

"Back away slowly," said Jack.

But Gordon seemed to be frozen in his shoes. His eyes bulged, and his mouth fell open as he stared at the bear.

Then the bear began to lumber heavily toward them.

"Come on!" urged Jack. At last Gordon
moved. He dodged behind Jack and raced
toward the nearest tree, dropping the
camera in his haste.

Jack turned to follow Gordon, but he didn't notice a hole hidden in the ground. Catching his foot in it, he fell heavily to the ground. A sharp pain shot through his ankle.

Terrified, he looked back to see that the bear was now running toward him like a huge, furry brown monster. Jack could see its angry eyes and long, sharp claws.

Jack yelled wildly, "Help me, Gordon! I can't get up!"

But Gordon, who had reached the foot of a tree, took one look at the bear and left Jack to his fate as he scrambled up the tree and out of the bear's reach.

Jack knew he was suppose to back away slowly, but since he'd hurt his ankle, all he could do was lie as still as possible and hope that the bear would leave him alone. He closed his eyes and waited.

The bear stopped, and Jack could sense its huge, warm bulk standing over him. He didn't dare move a muscle or twitch an eyelid. For a few miserable minutes, Jack felt the bear's hot breath on his face as the great beast sniffed all around him. Jack's nose began to itch, but he couldn't scratch it. He was too terrified even to breathe.

But at last, after what seemed an eternity, the bear moved away, and Jack heard it lumbering off into the forest. Only then did Jack open his eyes.

Breathing an enormous sigh of relief, Jack sat up. He struggled to his feet, relieved to find that his ankle was not quite as badly hurt as he had feared. Gordon slid down from the tree and hurried over to Jack.

"I'm OK, I can walk," said Jack as he turned away and began to hobble back the way they had come.

"That's good," said Gordon, picking up his camera and following after him. Then with a nervous laugh, he said, "Of course, I knew you'd be OK."

Jack said nothing.

After a moment Gordon tried again. "You know, when that bear was sniffing you, it looked as if it was whispering in your ear!" And he laughed again, as if he had made a great joke.

"It was," said Jack.

Gordon stopped laughing and looked at him in astonishment. "Really?" he gasped. "What did it say?"

"It told me to beware of friends who leave you when things get tough!" said Jack.

Gordon just turned a shameful shade of red and said, "Oh."